# The Martial Application of the Shotgun

By

## Paul G. Markel

The Martial Application of the Shotgun 2

# The Martial Application of the Shotgun

Paul G. Markel

Copr. 2022

All Rights Reserved

*No part of this text may be reproduced without the express written permission of the author and publisher.*

Cover Design: Zachary J. Markel

# Foreword

The first shotgun that I ever fired was a Harrington & Richardson 20 gauge single shot, breech loading gun that my parents purchased when we first moved onto our small family farm in rural Holmes County, Ohio. The first creature I ever took with said-gun was a cottontail rabbit. I skinned it out and my mother cooked it much like you would a chicken.

My best friend, Wayne, had a Sear & Roebuck "Ted Williams" 12 gauge, pump-action with a long vent rib barrel that belonged to his father. We boys had ready access to that gun and it would be the first 12G that I ever fired. Back then no one feared teenagers having access to rifles and shotguns. We were schooled in basic gun safety and we were not a bunch of prescription drugged-out sociopaths.

Of course, shotgun ammunition was far more expensive than .22 LR, so we naturally spent more recreational time in the woods with our rimfire guns, but we did take a fair amount of birds, rabbits, and squirrels with field loads fired from our shotguns.

Many of my peers went deer hunting with their fathers and fired slugs. Neither Wayne's dad nor mine were deer hunters, so our use of slugs was rare. We satisfied our ballistic need with the #7 or #9 birdshot/field loads.

When I was 18 years old I bought a Winchester Model 1200 "Defender" shotgun from The Gun Shop in Wooster, Ohio. The day I purchased the gun, the owner, Nick, advised me, "If you are going to practice, you can use game load, but if you want to load it up 'for real' you need these." Nick placed two, five-round boxes of Winchester 00 Buckshot on the counter and I dutifully purchased them. That would be my first experience with the high-brass, 00 buck. Slugs and buckshot were comparatively expensive to the birdshot I could get at every discount and hardware store, so I did not fire very many rounds of the buckshot.

During my time with the Security Forces Battalion in the US Marine Corp, I was introduced to the Remington Model 870 pump-action shotgun. When we trained with these Vietnam-era blasters, all we fired was GI-issued 00 buckshot. The Remington guns had 18 inch barrels and were made of steel and hardwood. About halfway through my tour of duty with the Security Forces, the Corps switched over to the Mossberg Model 590A1. I recall the new 590's looking more advanced and modern then our aged Remingtons. The new Mossberg guns held 7 shots in the magazine tube, as compared to only 4 shots in the Remingtons. They also had black polymer furniture. We young Marines felt "high speed" carrying the new Mossbergs on patrol.

However, back in the 1980's and 90's, we carried our guns a lot, but did not shoot them very often. During my entire active duty tour in the Marine Corps I might have fired 200 rounds of 00 buck from a shotgun, that is stretched out over four years.

It was not until I went through the Police Academy that I had a thorough, immersive training experience with a fighting shotgun. Back then, the 12 gauge, pump shotgun was found in every patrol car. This was long before we ever thought of such a thing as a "patrol rifle". In the Academy, we fired hundreds of rounds of birdshot as well as 00 buckshot and slugs. It was during this time that I truly gained an understanding of how 00 buck spread at various fighting distances.

One of my instructors explained to us that, "When fired from a cylinder bore gun, you can expect 00 buckshot to spread a half to one inch per yard." To demonstrate, our instructors set up a typical "hostage" paper target, the one where only the bad guy's head could be seen over the hostage's shoulder. An instructor stepped back three yards or so, took aim and fired. All nine 00 buck pellets went into one ragged hole that might have been two inches in diameter at the most. That demonstration stuck with me.

Having been trained with a 12 gauge fighting gun, I understood that most of the mythology surrounding the shotgun was just that, gun shop bullshit. Shotguns don't fill the air with dozens of screaming hornets of death making it "impossible" to miss.

During this book we will address the pros and cons of the fighting or combat shotgun as well as dispelling many of the popular myths that have been around for decades, if not centuries. A good friend of mine once opined, "People think of the shotgun as a beginner's or an amateur's gun. The truth is, if you are going to use one for fighting, the shotgun is actually the professional's choice."

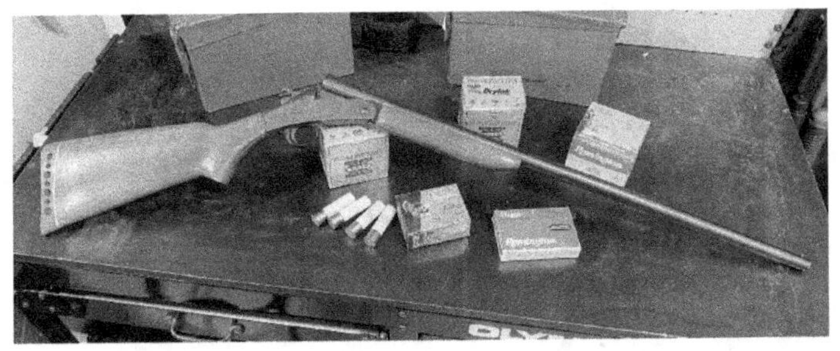

The author's first shotgun; an H&R "Topper" 20 gauge single-shot breech loader.

Please go to www.SOTGU.com for more information about shotgun and other training courses.

# Contents

# Introduction

The main function of this introduction is to establish the primary purpose of this text and to clarify our mission. Firearms can be enjoyed by many people and used for myriad purposes. If you are an American citizen, the right to possess arms is a birthright that no politician has the authority to deny you, although many will never stop trying.

If you live in any country besides the United States of America, firearms ownership is a regulated privilege and an expensive one at that. For socialist/authoritarian nations, charging large fees for the privilege to own a gun is par for the course. In our world, prior to the United States, it was always the wealthy elitists, and of course the governments who stole the people's money via taxes, who could afford to possess arms.

Throughout the history of firearms, they have been used in hunting, in competitions or games, collected as objects of affection, used by governments to defeat their enemies and oppress their citizens, and lastly in the interest of self-defense and to stand against tyranny.

At Student of the Gun, we have asserted from the beginning that a firearm, a gun, must always be considered an *Instrument of Liberty* by free men, citizens not slaves. The moment you first view a gun as a tool used for recreation, for hunting, for engaging in games and sport, you lose the understanding as to why the Citizens of the United States were assured the unalienable right to possess arms.

American citizens have many unalienable rights, but they do not have a "right" to hunt *(hunting is not once mentioned in the US Constitution)*, to play games, or to collect objects for recreation. The only right to keep and bear arms comes from the unalienable right to protect *LIFE and LIBERTY.*

Regarding shotguns, there are certainly many enjoyable recreational activities that you can engage in and that is all well and good. The reason that I choose to title this book "The Martial Application of the Shotgun" is to make clear that our focus herein is not sports or recreation, but the use of a shotgun as a tool to defend both Life and Liberty from those who would seek to take either or both.

It is true that certain principles and fundamentals crossover between fighting with a shotgun or shooting a match or even taking game in hunting. Fundamental marksmanship applies to all because the gun is inanimate, it does not know nor care for which purpose it is being used. However, there will be times when the application and tactical employment that we recommend will vary from what might be common in recreation or games. With that being said, please continue.

*"This is the law. The purpose of fighting is to win. There is no possible victory in defense. The sword is more important than the shield, and skill is more important than either. The final weapon is the brain. All else is supplementary."*
*~John Steinbeck*

***Author's Note: As always, it is recommended that prior to reading this book that you grab a pencil for notetaking and a highlighter of some sort.**

# Chapter 1 The Martial Application of the Shotgun

The 12 gauge shotgun is one of the most prevalent firearms in the United States, if not the world. Even socialist shitholes that forbid the ownership of handguns and rifles often allow their peasant tax slaves to own fowling pieces because the tyrant state views them as quaint or rather innocuous.

In the United States, Remington Arms has sold over 11 million Model 870 shotguns and O.F. Mossberg is close behind with over 10 million variations of the Model 500 shotgun sold. Folks, that's over 20 million shotguns, not including other brands such as Benelli, Ithaca, Winchester, Browning, and innumerable smaller makers in the hands of American citizens.

When addressing the use of a shotgun from a martial perspective, one of the biggest obstacles is also one of the biggest selling points of the shotgun. Shotguns have so many uses; sports, recreational hunting for both small and large game, self-defense, combat, etc. that there can be a good deal of confusion for the end user. Federal Ammunition lists over

50 different 12 gauge loads on their official website. They have shells from the currently popular 1 ¾ inch "shorty shells" up to 3 ½ inch magnum loads. It is no wonder that the end user can be overwhelmed by all the choices.

For this text, we will focus strictly on the use of a shotgun as a fighting or martial tool. That will help us to cut down on much of the confusion. If you desire to shoot clays, birds, geese, deer or ducks that is fantastic and fun, but this is not our aim here. Our mission is to prepare ourselves to deal with two legged threats.

As far back as the Colonial era of the United States, prudent men understood that a 12 gauge "scattergun" or "fowling piece" was a devastating close quarters weapon in the hands of a trained shooter. During the great Western expansion, men chopped down the 24 and 28 inch barrels on their fowling pieces to create guns that were far easier to maneuver and bring to bear. The "Coach Gun" was born and a mythology grew around it. This was both good and bad as much of the popular mythology regarding "you can't miss with a shotgun" began around that time. The nickel and dime novels that were produced during that era only served to spread the legend of the Coach Gun.

We have certainly come a long way since the flint or caplock scatterguns and paper shells that the "Shotgun Messenger" carried on the Wells Fargo stagecoaches. However, the function of the shotgun has essentially remained the same.

The shotgun in a martial role was and has remained a close quarters fighting tool. Yes, we can use slugs to extend the range, but even these huge chunks of lead have their limitations as gravity pulls them to the ground.

Despite advances in rifles and submachine guns, the 12 gauge shotgun has seen service in every major conflict the United States has been in. The Marine Corps famously used the Winchester Model 1897 pump-action shotgun in World War I and it was dubbed "the trench gun". The weapon was used to such devastating effect that the Germans once declared that using a shotgun was "barbarous" and threatened to execute any man captured with a shotgun or even shotgun ammunition on his person as a "war criminal". To that threat, an American General responded that if the

Germans did so, every German soldier captured would be executed on the spot. History tells us that the Germans decided not to carry out their threat.

While serving in the Marine Corps Infantry, one of the NCO's in my company used to relate a story that was passed down from his father who was a Marine Infantryman in Vietnam. The way he explained it, his father told him, "Of all the sounds of combat; rifles, machine guns, grenades, when we heard the distinctive sound of a shotgun firing, we knew that someone just got fucked up."

Later on, while working as a Military Contractor during GWOT, I had a man on my team who had been a Marine Corps Machine Gun Section Leader. The weapon he was issued was a Benelli M4 12 gauge autoloader. The man had fought in the battle of Fallujah and related to me that he would never carry any other gun for close quarters, house to house fighting.

Even admitting the fact that a shotgun is a close quarters tool, it is not that much of a detriment as mortal combat encounters all tend to be relatively fast and violent affairs where only a few yards separate the combatants. Herein lies another misunderstanding of the shotgun.

During the era of the police or patrol shotgun, there were many under-trained men who had the belief that handguns were for close encounters, but they might go for the shotgun if they believed the threat would be a bit farther off. I had one veteran officer tell me that "A shotgun is no good inside a house, there is not enough room to maneuver."

Such thinking is sophistry. The shotgun is a powertool for fighting, not a distance tool. Think of it like this. If you needed to knock down a brick wall or smash cinder blocks and you had the choice, would you grab a one pound claw hammer or a five pound sledgehammer? Yes, with enough time and effort, you could break a cinder block with a carpenter's hammer, but would it not make more sense to use a sledgehammer?

We need to think of the 12 gauge shotgun as a sledgehammer. Claw hammers are lighter and easier to carry, but a sledgehammer is going to do a far better job smashing or destroying what needs to be broken. Would you rather hit a cinder block ten times with a carpenter's hammer or once with a 5-pound sledge?

A decade or so previous, I was in a tactical/fighting shotgun class. The instructor offered some words of advice. "The fighting shotgun is one of the most misunderstood tools in the inventory. People either assume they cannot miss or they overthink it. When I look at a 12 gauge pump gun, I think of it like a pit bull, like a guard dog. It is ferocious and mean and it is constantly hungry. If you are not shooting your gun you should be feeding it." I could find no fault in that description and those words have stuck with me to this day.

As we progress throughout this text, that is how we are going to view the fighting shotgun, as a sledgehammer or a pit bull, a guard dog. Your cocker spaniel might bark a lot and be able to bite, but wouldn't you rather that a cracked-out home invader face down a 75 pound German Shepherd?

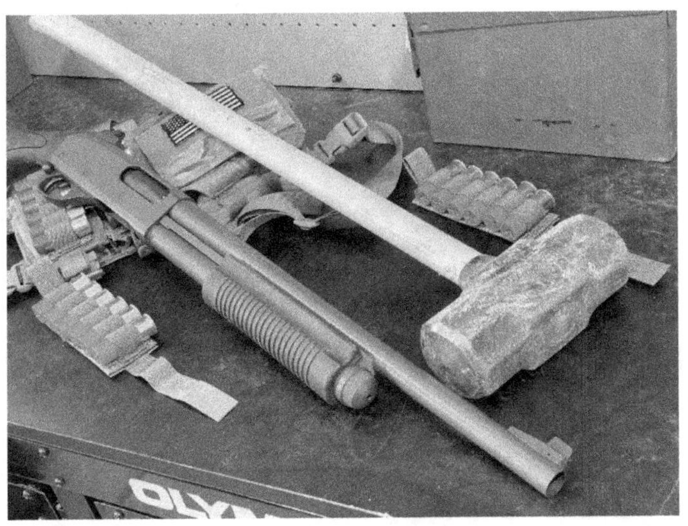

**Consider the 12 gauge fighting shotgun as
a self-defense sledge hammer.**

# Chapter 2 Why the 12 Gauge?

Returning to the subject of end user confusion, there are many pundits and gun shop "experts" that would say that a 20 gauge or even a .410 is a better home defense gun. They buttress this argument by saying that either of the aforementioned "kick-less" or are "easier to handle".

Yes, is it better to have "a gun" in your hands than no gun when facing a deadly threat, but the fact of the matter is that the 12 gauge offers more options and solutions than the others. Even rural gas stations and hardware stores are likely to have 12 gauge ammunition in stock all of the time and dedicated personal defense ammunition in 12 gauge abounds.

Regarding the 12 gauge, as it is viewed not just as a sporting tool, but a fighting instrument, there are far more loads designed for combat than any of the others. While we are on the subject, if you are going to be an intelligent shooter, you should know where the term "gauge" originated as opposed to "caliber".

The gauge of a shotgun has for centuries been determined by the number of round lead balls of that diameter which will equal one Imperial pound. So, it takes 12 round lead balls of that diameter to equal a pound for a 12 gauge. A 16 gauge shotgun means that it takes sixteen round lead balls, etc. The original 16 gauge ball/slug weighed 1 ounce. The original 12 gauge ball or slug weighed 1 and ¼ ounce of lead. The 10 gauge, quite a monster, but rare today, fired 1 and ½ ounce slugs. The .410 is not a true "gauge" it is a "caliber". Our lesson here is that when it comes to gauge, the smaller the number, the larger the bore diameter.

Ironically, or purposefully, the same applies to the size of shot fired from a shotgun. You see, 00 buckshot is larger than #4 buckshot or BB's. Field loads are the same; #6 shot is larger than #9 shot. Modern slug ammunition does not always follow the old rules. While the old "Foster" type 12 gauge slugs were a true 1 ¼ ounce of lead, many modern 12 gauge slugs weigh an even ounce. When it comes to 00 buckshot, a typical 12 gauge shell contains 9 projectiles, but there are 8 pellet loads available.

*Author's Note: The genius of the Foster slug is that the rifling is built into the slug itself so it *can be fired down the smooth bore of a shotgun and still fly straight.*

**Federal's 12 gauge ammo game is strong.**

Not to confuse you too much, but 00 buckshot is the standard. The 0 buck is smaller and the 000 buck is larger. A #4 buckshot is much smaller than 00 buckshot. To reduce end user confusion, for our purposes, we will focus on 00 buckshot and slugs for fighting and field loads or birdshot for much higher round count, training endeavors.

Additionally, when it comes to the 12 gauge buckshot load, you will encounter both the sporting or hunting variety and the designated law enforcement or personal defense varieties. The sporting ammunition is what you will find on the shelves of your local discount or hardware stores. Law enforcement/personal defense 00 buckshot is loaded to be a bit softer or slower thus offering less felt recoil while still driving the pellets faster than 1000 feet per second.

Also, you will encounter the terms "low brass" and "high brass". The brass portion of the shotgun shell is where the propellant powder is contained. A birdshot or field load does not require as much powder and therefore has less felt recoil than a "high brass" round of buckshot or a slug. Low brass translates practically to lower felt recoil and high brass translates to higher felt recoil. Fear not, high brass shells are NOT going to dislocate your shoulder.

**12 gauge shotgun shells
(L to R) 1 ¾", 2 ¾", 3" and 3 ½".**

# Chapter 3      Shotgun Actions

Now that we have settled on the 12 as the preferred gauge for martial use and we understand that we use a shotgun as a powertool, not a distance or precision instrument, let's consider the various actions available.

While there might be some debate about which action is the most prevalent in the United States, considering our previous discussion of both Remington and Mossberg production rates, there are well over 20 million pump action 12 gauge shotguns in circulation in the good old USA.

## Pump Action

The "pump" or "slide" action shotgun has attributes and detriments. The attributes would include a relatively simple, straightforward manual of arms. Also, because a slide-action gun is manually operated, they are not generally ammunition sensitive. Most standard 12 gauge slide-action guns are chambered to accept up to 3 inch shells.

Also, the pump action shotgun is a "repeating firearm". We don't use that term much today, but that means it can be fired multiple times without the need to be reloaded. Depending on the brand and model, your pump gun might start out with four plus one, or seven plus one or even more.

Economy is another attribute. The pump action 12 gauge shotgun is a time tested design and it is relatively inexpensive for modern manufacturers to produce. Depending on the model, you could purchase two, perhaps three, pump action shotguns for the price of a single, self-loading rifle. If you have a tight budget, but need to arm several people, the 12 gauge pump is an attractive option.

The primary downside or detriment to a slide-action shotgun is the requirement to use two hands to operate it *(Ed Mireles and Sarah Connor aside)*. In our modern world of semi-auto handguns and rifles, manually working the action on a firearm can truly be a foreign undertaking to many folks. You cannot just hand a pump shotgun to a novice or an untrained person and simply expect them to figure it out. Well, they might figure it out eventually, but that is not the best way to go about it.

**Mossberg 590S**

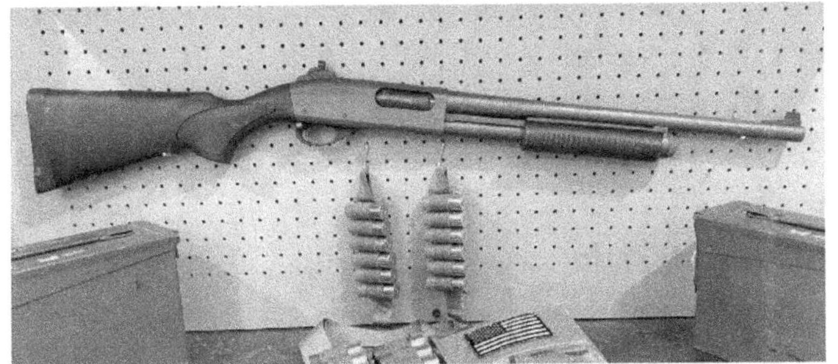

**Remington 870**

## Semi-Automatic

The semi-automatic or gas-operated shotgun is an attractive option to many shooters. Gas operated guns have also been referred to as autoloaders. Since John Browning's famous "Auto 5", gas guns have come a long way.

The attributes of the semi-auto 12 gauge are pretty obvious; once loaded the gun keeps on shooting shot after shot with the press of the trigger, no pumping required. The manual of arms for loading is generally a simple affair; stuff the magazine tube full, work the action to chamber a round and you are off and running. Gas guns will cycle very fast which can be both a benefit and a detriment. It's cool to fire five shorts in two seconds, but you also should appreciate the reality that your gun will be empty rather quickly.

For the modern shooter who is used to using semi-auto pistols and rifles, using a semi-auto shotgun is a natural transition. Depending on the model in question, the learning curve can be short. The detriment with gas guns has always been ammo sensitivity. Benelli USA has the gas issue all figured out, their semi-auto guns will run birdshot, buckshot and slugs all without missing a beat. That is great.

The Benelli guns will also set you back $1500 to $2000 per unit. Many of the less expensive or more economical gas guns have adjustable gas systems for low brass or high brass. I have a Mossberg 930 Tactical shotgun and it will run field loads as well as high brass, but even that model will set you back better than $1000.

If you decide on a gas-operated shotgun, whether tube fed or magazine fed, you must test out the ammunition you are planning to use in the gun and be sure it will cycle reliably.

**VP 12 magazine-fed semi-auto**

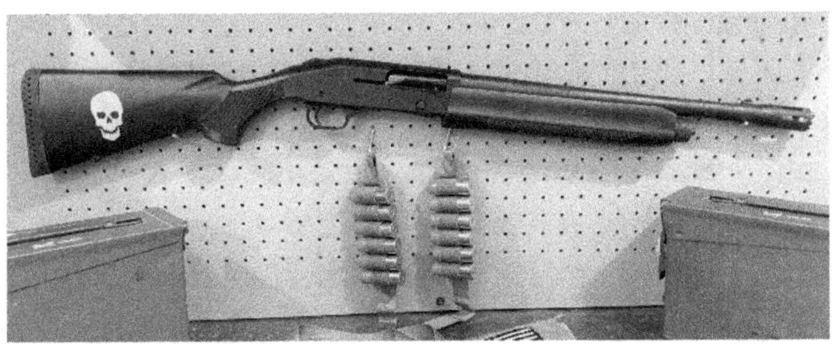

**Mossberg 930 tube-fed semi-auto**

**Breech Loading**

The breech loading or "break-action" shotgun is the classic design we all grew up seeing on movies or TV. The typical break-action uses either a single or a double-barrel. The double barrel, break-action, is likely the most famous because that was the model that became the Coach Gun.

Attributes for the breech loading gun are naturally ease of operation and straight forward manual of arms. Break action guns fall into two basic categories; exposed hammer or concealed hammer. The exposed hammer variety is found on most all inexpensive single barreled shotguns. Double-guns with exposed hammers might look cool but they are the least desirable of the two options for a fighting gun.

There are Triple-barreled breech loading shotguns out there. However, they are relatively rare and rather expensive.

The detriments of a breech loading shotgun are both limited ammunition capacity and the time and effort required to load them again. With a breech loading gun we go back to the idea that having "a gun" is better than not, but there are far better options available to us.

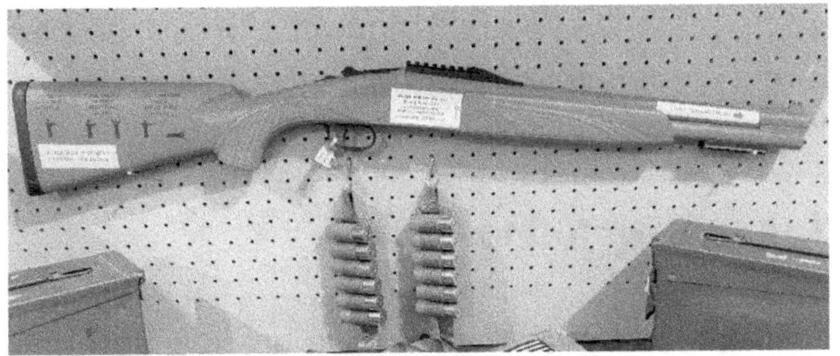

**Maverick 12 over/under breechloader.
When you only have 2 shells, you need to
make them count.**

## Decisions

So, which gun do we recommend for your use as a combat shotgun? If you have the budget, a semi-automatic shotgun from a reliable manufacturer is a good option. Though, from a practical standpoint, if you were planning to spend $1000 to $2000 on a long gun to use as a fighting tool, wouldn't that money be better spent on an AR or even an FN FAL/SA58? It is your money, spend it however you desire.

From the most traditional or classic standpoint, the slide-action 12 gauge shotgun is relatively inexpensive, robust, and will cycle most any ammunition you can find, from super-light trap loads to heavy hitting buck and slugs. Also, pump guns, while not falling off of trees, can be found everywhere. Even the pussies at Walmart still sell 12 gauge pump guns.

## To Choke or Not to Choke

Another option that the  shotgun has and one that causes some confusion with novice and experienced shooters alike is; What choke should I use? Or do I need a choke? A shotgun choke can be either a permanent part of the barrel or screwed in. The purpose of the choke is to restrict or tighten the pattern of shot as it exits the barrel.

The basic types of chokes are; improved, modified, full, and cylinder bore. I know there are others, save your letters. A cylinder bore means that no additional choking was added. **Improved** is a slight choke, **modified** is more or the medium, and **full** is, well, the most or tightest.

In regards to using a shotgun as a fighting tool, the simple answer is that you do not need a choke. It is generally inadvisable or a bad idea to shoot solid projectiles *(slugs)* through barrels with screw-in chokes. For your fighting gun, you want to be able to shoot field loads, buckshot and slugs without having to change or modify the gun. The vast majority of 12 gauge shotguns built and sold as defensive guns have cylinder bore barrels.

## Patterning

While we are thinking about chokes and patterns or spread, let's talk about test patterning your fighting shotgun with whichever load you are going to purchase for defense. Regarding low brass birdshot or field loads for training, you don't really need to worry about patterning. However, with 00 buckshot or even slugs, you definitely want to know what is happening on the receiving end of the shotgun.

Patterning is not difficult. All you need is your gun, the ammo you have chosen for defensive use, and cardboard or paper with some kind of backer. I like to use the generic cardboard silhouette targets, but a discarded pizza box will work in a pinch.

One of the first questions you need to answer for yourself is; How far is a realistic distance to test my shotgun? If you are using a shotgun as a home defense weapon, consider your house. How long is the longest straight shot that you could take inside of your home? You can pace it off or use a tape measure if you are really OCD. Unless you live in a mansion or a warehouse, I would venture to say that an unobstructed shot inside of your home will be no longer than ten yards, maybe fifteen if you have long hallways.

Once you have the distance of the longest shot that you might be expected to take, hit the range with your gear. Set up your target, pace off the distance you recorded from your home, take steady aim at the center and let one fly. Assess your shot and be honest, were you holding the muzzle steady? If so, go check out the pattern. If you are using 00 buckshot, count the holes. Some of the holes might be oblong because two pieces of shot made one big hole.

What you see is what you get. This is the size of the shot pattern that you can regularly expect from that particular gun using that particular load. Most people who have never done this exercise are a bit surprised at how tight the pattern actually is. Remember, the standard spread is only ½ to 1 inch per yard from a cylinder bore gun with 00 buckshot.

If you have decided to load slugs in your home defense gun, I would recommend taking a black marker and making a two-inch dot in the upper chest area. Steady the gun and slow-fire 3 shots of slugs at the dot from the prescribed distance. This pattern will let you know how on or off your sights are. This is particularly important if your shotgun has only a brass bead for an aiming indicator. Again, you might be surprised or very pleased at the results.

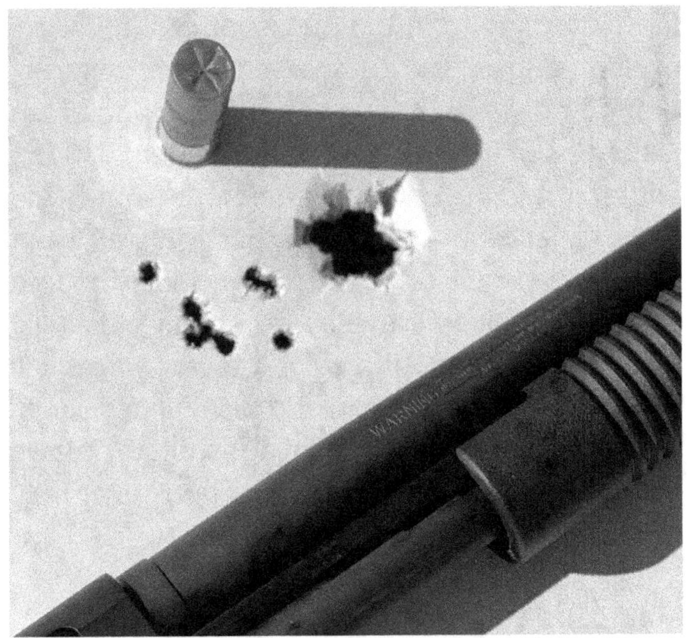

**00 Buck pattern fired from 7 yards with a cylinder bore choke.**
**(large hole is from the wad)**

*Keep in mind, the plastic or cardboard wad that separates the powder from the projectiles is going to make a mark or hole in your target. Disregard the wad hole or tear in the target. Some folks get confused by this when they fire a slug and two holes appear in the cardboard. Close examination will let you know which was which.

In the case that you are displeased with either the patterning from the buckshot or the impact of the slugs, you can purchase a different brand or style of 00 buck or you can add some kind of sighting system to your gun. If your shotgun has no option for different sights, you have a decision to make. Either live with what you have or get something new. Most modern shotgun receivers have as an option the ability to add a scope/optic rail. Many people will install a 1:1 red dot optic and dial it in for slugs. A magnified optic on fighting shotgun slows down target acquisition and is truly unnecessary.

**Magazine Fed Shotguns**

Before we move on to the next chapter, let's consider the currently popular trend of the magazine fed shotgun. Both pump action and gas operated 12 gauge shotguns can be had with detachable magazines. At first glance, the magazine fed shotgun seems like a great idea. When you run out, rather than stuff rounds one at a time into the gun, you can simply insert a magazine of five, maybe ten, rounds in a matter of a couple of seconds. Speed and ease of loading is a big selling point for magazine fed shotguns. There is no doubt about that.

Now here is the reality check. Shotgun magazines are large, I would go so far as to say they are "extra large". Even a .308 magazine pouch is too small to carry them. Five round, 12 gauge magazines are manageable, ten round magazines give you 10+1 before you need to load again, but they are huge.

I have found that a US Military SAW pouch will hold four 5 round magazines. If you want to carry the 10 round magazines, a sling bag or single-strap, over-the-shoulder bag is probably the way to go. The benefit of a tube fed magazine is that you don't have to worry about losing or carrying magazines. Also, in a hurry, a pump-action, tube fed gun can be quickly loaded by dropping a single round to the open action.

I am not trying to talk you out of a magazine loaded shotgun. However, if that is what you want to use, you need to consider how you are going to carry extra magazines.

The big drum magazines for shotguns, 15 or 20 rounds, sure do look sexy on videos, but those bastards are heavy and many of the off-brand models have serious reliability issues. Let the buyer beware.

**Magazine-fed shotguns offer convenient loading, but the magazines are a pain to carry around.**

**Rather than being "too unwieldy" for indoor use, the shotgun is a power tool used to protect your home.**

# Chapter 4 Training: Running the Machine

Training with a shotgun encompasses the same confusion pitfalls as does choosing the action and the ammunition for the tool. The first issue that Small Arms Instructors will encounter is the perception that 'no one needs to train with a shotgun'. Afterall, you just 'point it and pull the trigger'. I was present when a man was advising others in regard to firing a shotgun for defense. The man said to the group, "Inside of ten yards you can't miss with a shotgun. Don't waste time shouldering the gun. Just fire it from your hip."

I was merely an observer to this farce, so I stood back and watched a dozen shooters fire 00 buckshot from the hip at cardboard silhouette targets. What I witnessed were shots going above, below, to the left and to the right of the targets. Most of the shooters only managed to get a few pellets onto the cardboard.

If you have already gone through the patterning exercise for your fighting gun or if you just read what we discussed about pellet spread, you will realize that what that jackass said about being close and "you can't miss" is the opposite of correct. The closer you are, the more important it is for the muzzle to be indexed on the target.

**Universal Firearms Safety Rules**

The 4 Universal Firearms Safety Rules are;

1) *Treat All Guns as if they are loaded all the time.*

2) *Keep your finger straight and off the trigger until the sights are aligned and you've made the decision to fire.*

3) *Never allow the muzzle to cover anything you are not willing to destroy.*

4) *Know your target*, what is around it and what is beyond it.

These rules are called *universal* because they apply everywhere in the known universe. That means we follow them on the range, in our house, at the gun shop, and even during a life or death encounter. There are far more things in the world which should not be shot than things that should be.

## Martial Training

In the United States, there are numerous schools where you can go to learn how to shoot a shotgun for sport. Trap, skeet, 5 Stand, Sporting Clays are all enjoyable sports and I have had the pleasure to participate in all of them over the years. Nonetheless, when we choose training for our fighting scattergun, we need to go back to the power tool discussion or the pit bull/guard dog focus.

A fighting shotgun is a powerful tool and it is always hungry. If you are not shooting it you need to be feeding it. Also, as a powerful tool, you are either going to control the gun or it is going to control you. By that I mean, we have all likely witnessed people shooting shotguns where it appears as if the gun is beating them up or controlling them.

When it comes to training with a martial shotgun we need to focus on…
   1) The Mount and Stockweld
   2) Working the Action
   3) Feeding the Beast

*… Let's break these down one at a time.*

## Mount

By the mount we mean getting the gun into place on our body with your dominant and support hands in the correct position and the butt of the stock placed firmly into the shoulder pocket area. Many novice shooters will be afraid of the gun and try to keep it off of their shoulder. Their reward for this behavior is a pounding and good sized purple bruise.

When we bring the stock up to your shoulder pocket we place it firmly against our body and lean into the gun by putting our shoulders out in front of our hips. Regarding stance, your feet should be about shoulder width apart, toes pointing forward, weight on the center foot, not the toes or the heels.

The dominant hand will grip either a pistol grip or the grip portion of a traditional stock. Your support hand has a firm hold on the forearm or forend, ready to pump the action the moment the shot breaks.

Stockweld is also referred to as cheek weld, this is the place that your cheek will make contact with the comb *(top)* of the stock. Like the shoulder issue, novice shooters will try to keep their cheek off the stock just a little bit. Again, their reward is a smack in the face. Instead, we will place our cheek so that it touches the comb of the stock with our cheekbone just above. A good stockweld will put your dominant eye in direct line with the bore of the gun. Whether you have rifle style sights or a simple brass bead out front, a proper stockweld will put your dominant eye right where it needs to be for rapid target acquisition.

Another portion of the mounting process will be to disengage the *manual safety* on the gun. Depending on the make and model, the location of the manual safety will vary. For the Mossberg 500 series, the safety lever is on the tang, in the center, making it ambidextrous. We use our dominant thumb to engage and disengage the Mossberg safety. For the Remington 870 series, and many others, the safety is a cross bolt design located in the rear of the trigger guard. To disengage the Remington safety you push it from right to left and then left to right to engage. Right handed shooters will use their index finger to disengage and their thumb to engage.

Many novice shooters never learn how to properly manipulate the safety, or at least how to manipulate it rapidly, because they never chamber a round until they plan to fire the gun. They just leave the safety in the **off** position all the time and chamber a round by pressing the action release lever.

There are a couple of reasons why this is a bad habit. First, the shotgun is a relatively low-capacity gun to begin with. If you are using a standard 870 Police Model, the magazine tube holds 4 shells and the chamber holds 1 more. When you keep the chamber empty in this case you are reducing your ammunition capacity by 20 percent!

Another reason that the empty chamber/safety off situation is a poor choice is that sooner or later, the safety will be in the on position when you find yourself trying to shoot and the gun will not fire. People who never practice engaging the manual safety will freeze and go into a temporary vapor lock trying to figure out why the gun didn't fire. If you are in the middle of a fight for your life, this can be a deadly mistake.

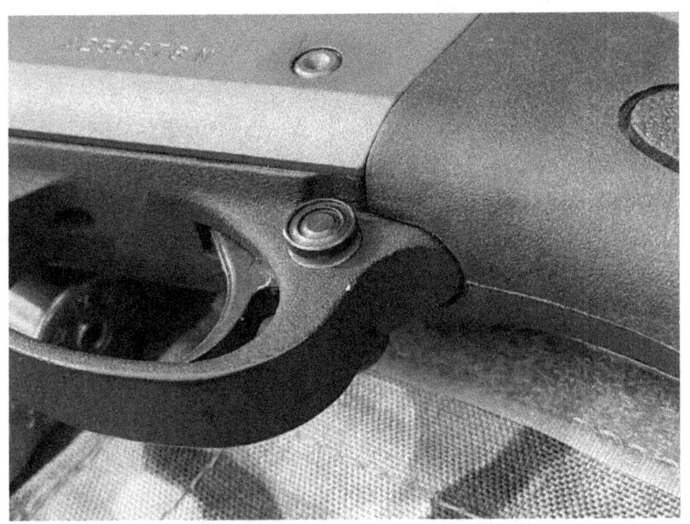

**Remington 870 crossbolt safety**

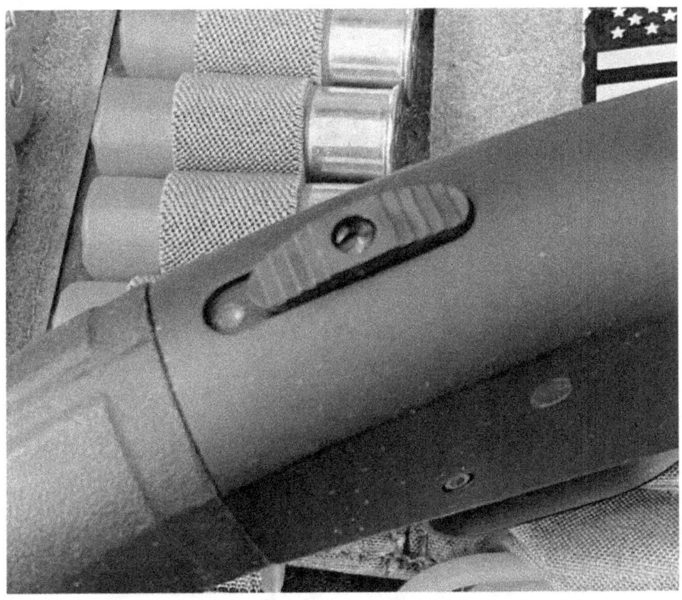

**Mossberg 590 ambi safety**

## Working the Action

For this section we will assume that the shooter is using some type of pump or slide action gun. Remember, a pump action shotgun is manually operated, you have to do the work. When the bolt/action is in the forward position, it is locked in place. To unlock the action, we either depress the action release lever or we press the trigger. Being professionals who do NOT snap the trigger reflexively, the only time we press the trigger is when we are intending to shoot the gun. For administrative chores; loading, unloading, clearing the chamber, we will use the action release lever.

The action release lever is located on the forward portion of the Remington 870 trigger guard. On the Mossberg 500 series, the action release lever is found at the rearward or back portion of the trigger guard.

Remember, the trigger action on a pump shotgun is *single*, that is, the trigger's only job is to release the firing pin. The average factory trigger press weight on a shotgun designed for self-defense/fighting will be around 7 pounds. This is perfectly fine. We do not need to worry about aftermarket "match" or "target" triggers.

When engaging targets, the moment the shot breaks, the shooter will vigorously work the pump action by drawing the forearm back as far as it will travel and then vigorously pushing it forward until it stops and the action locks. This process both removes the expended shotshell and grabs a fresh round to be chambered. One of the most common problems that new or novice shotgun shooters have is failing to work the action vigorously and deliberately. In the training business we call this error "short stroking the gun". Short stroking will clear the chamber, but the action does not pick up a fresh round.

The bolt and the action bars are made of tempered steel, you do not need to baby them or treat them gently. On most new pump action shotguns, the actions tend to be a bit stiff and the gun will smooth out and run better the more often you vigorously run the action rails back and forth.

When we are training to fight with a shotgun, we will run the action while the gun is still mounted on our shoulder. Removing the butt from the shoulder to operate that action is a complete waste of time in a mortal combat situation. Once we have mounted the gun, we do not remove it from our shoulders until we have made the conscious decision that no additional shots are needed.

With a determined effort and focus on working the action, shooters will be able to deliver multiple shots rapidly onto a single or multiple targets. Two shots in two seconds using 00 buckshot was the law enforcement standard for qualification when I was a police officer.

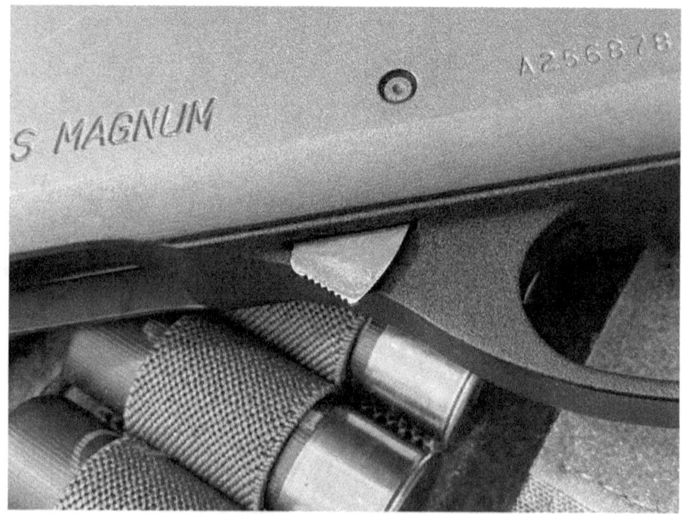


**Remington 870 slide release**

**Mossberg 590 slide release**

## Feeding

Keep in mind our mantra, *if you are not shooting your gun, you should be feeding it.* In order to keep your 12 gauge guard dog well-fed, you need to pre-plan or have ammunition staged where you can readily reach it. There are many ways and methods to carry extra shotgun ammunition. One of the most popular is the side saddle shell holder that affixes to the receiver of the shotgun on the side opposite the ejection port. Side saddle shell holders generally hold 4 to 6 additional shells. There are also numerous styles of shell carriers which affix to the buttstock of the gun.

**Side Saddle shell holder**

Some people will use shell loops mounted on a belt or carried in a bandolier fashion. Still others will use a pouch of some sort carried on the support side of the body. However you decide to carry extra shells, you need to practice retrieving this ammunition and feeding your gun.

Original SOE Gear has a dedicated shotgun ammunition carrier called the "12 Gauge Micro Rig". This dedicated chest carrier will hold 24 rounds of 12 gauge shells in loops and it has a large axillary pouch for a trauma kit or anything you desire.

**SOE Gear Shotgun Micro Rig**

One of the fastest ways to load a pump action shotgun that has been fired dry is to open the action, retrieve a shell and drop it directly into the action via the eject port. The moment the support hand drops the shell into the action, it grabs the slide and runs it closed. The shooter now fires immediately if the situation calls for it.

For standard or traditional magazine tube feeding, the shooter will control the gun with their dominant hand and rotate it so that the feeding ramp/magazine tube is toward the support side. The support hand now stuffs shells into the tube until it will not accept any more. Again, depending on the model, this might be 4, 5, 6, or more if your gun is really long.

You will note that I said to feed shells into the magazine tube until it will not accept any more. I did not say to count your shells. Our aim in training is to prepare to function during the gravest extreme, a life or death encounter. If you just fired your shotgun at one or more potential killers, there will be a chemical cocktail pumping through your veins. Calmly counting out rounds as you load is going to be as close to impossible as you can get and you really don't need to even try.

That brings us to another valid point. During a fight for your life, you will not be able to count the shots you fire. You will fire rounds until either the threat is no longer there or the gun stops making noise. During the famous FBI Miami Shootout, Ed Mireles started with five 00 buckshot rounds in his Police Model 870. During the after action briefing, Ed stated that he only remembered firing four rounds, his gun was empty and there were five shotgun shells on the ground but, even years later, Ed could only remember firing four. This is extremely common, so much so as to be the rule. Officers involved in life and death shootings will say that they thought they fired "3 or 4" shots, but when they check their magazine, they realize that it is missing 7 or 8 rounds.

During the adrenaline fog of a fight for your life, you cannot be expected to keep track of the number of shots. The rule is that we shoot until the threat no longer remains. That could be one shot or two or five. You do not get to decide. Remember, your attacker gets a say as to when they are going to stop. Going back to the FBI Miami Shootout. William Matix was shot 6 times with 9mm and .38 Special +P before he stopped fighting and died. Michael Platt was shot 12 times with 9mm, .38 Special +P and 00 buckshot before he quit fighting and expired.

When you have decided that you do not need to continue shooting, stuff the magazine tube until it will not accept any more rounds and then run the action vigorously by depressing the action release lever. A round may eject onto the ground or the chamber might be empty, it does not matter. It is more important to ensure that the gun is loaded and ready to fire than it is to worry about a round on the ground. Whether a round falls out or does not, simply grab it or another round and stuff it into the magazine tube. Now you have a life saving tool that is ready to continue fighting if need be.

## Stoppages

The good news is that stoppages when using a slide-action shotgun are rare. However, we cannot ignore the fact that they sometimes do happen. The bad news is that a genuine stoppage like a Type 3 can be frustrating and time consuming.

### *Type 1*  *Failure to Fire (Click No Boom)*

The Type 1 stoppage or failure to fire with a slide action shotgun will occur 99 times out of 100 due to the shooter failing to load the chamber either because they neglected to do so or they short stroked the action. When using a tubular magazine gun, no tapping is needed. The solution to a Type 1 stoppage is to work/rack the slide vigorously and attempt to fire if necessary.

If the Type 1 occurred at the very beginning of the firing cycle, there should be plenty of ammunition in the gun. If you have been shooting for a while and the gun goes "click" no boom, it will likely be empty. Remember our mantra back in the beginning? If you are not shooting the gun you need to be feeding it.

### Type 2   *Feedway Obstruction/Stove-Pipe*

With slide/pump action guns, I have never seen or experienced a stove-pipe stoppage. I have witnessed them and experienced them with semi-automatic guns. If you have manually pumped the action and the offending shell has not fallen away, you will need to knock it out/off with your support hand.

For a Type 2 with a semi-auto shotgun, the support hand reaches under the gun as the dominant hand angles the ejection port toward the ground. Using the support hand, work the action vigorously. That should do it.

### Type 3        *Double Feed*

The Type 3 or double feed stoppage occurs in pump action shotguns 999 times out of 1000 because the shooter short-stroked the action. What you have now is either an empty shell and a fresh, new shell inside the action or two unfired shells. Either way, the gun is not going to work until you unfuck this situation.

Draw a Secondary Gun or Seek Cover.

Rack the slide back so that the action is open all the way. Rotate the ejection port to the ground and agitate the gun to help the offending shells fall away. Do not bother trying to catch them. Keep your dominant hand on the grip. If this does not work, the support hand fingers are going to have to get in and do some poking and prodding.

In some semi-automatic guns, a Type 3 is truly a motherfucker and requires a tool; knife, screwdriver, etc. to clear.

With the offending shells removed, vigorously work the action to load a fresh round and attempt to fire if necessary.

***Author's Note: If you are involved in a fight, the time it takes to clear a Type 3 will seem like an eternity. You either need cover if you do not have a secondary gun handy. If you are really close to your threat, you might consider hitting them with the shotgun.**

# Chapter 5 Martial Tactics

Mindset and Tactics are the two most important aspects of winning a deadly force encounter. During this section, we will consider the tactics that we will practice so that they will be employed during a martial or combat scenario. Mindset comes into play when the shooter decides to train and practice good tactics.

### *Carrying the Gun*

Keep in mind, we train on the range so that we can perform in the real world. There are firearms instructors that love to yell "keep you muzzle down range". Well, here is a reality check, out in the world, everything is down range or nothing is, depending on how you look at it. People who carry handguns for self-protection walk around in the world with their guns secured in a holster. The gun only comes out in the world when it is needed. When we carry a shotgun, we don't have a holster for it. The closest thing we have to a holster would be a sling. When we sling a long gun, it is normally for administrative carrying, when a fight is not perceived or is likely. *(We will address sling carry later on in this chapter)*

When we are carrying a shotgun out in the world; whether the world is our living room, our neighborhood, or out in the field somewhere, we need to be conscious of the direction in which our muzzle is pointed.

## Muzzle Down

Muzzle down with a shotgun is not all that different from muzzle down carry with a rifle or carbine. The dominant hand controls the gun by holding the grip area. The support hand holds the forend or slide portion of the gun. While the muzzle should not be pointed at our feet, it should also NOT be angled so that you are sweeping the knees and shins of everyone around you. A rule would be that your muzzle will point about twelve inches out from the center of your legs.

When carrying a shotgun in the muzzle down position, the gun will normally be rotated so that the receiver is flat against the body. For a right handed shooter, the ejection port will be facing out. For the left handed shooter, the ejection port will be rotated to face the body. The butt of the stock will be close to the shoulder pocket.

***Author's Note:** Yes, I understand that there are "left handed" shotguns out there. Nonetheless, they are in fact rare. For our purposes, we will consider that the shotgun you are using is a standard, right handed model.

To address a target from the muzzle down carry, we simply roll the butt up into the shoulder pocket. Since the butt is already very close to the mount position, this is a quick or rapid way to come on target and a skilled shooter can roll the gun up, disengage the manual safety, and come to mount for a shot in about one second.

**Muzzle Down Carry**

## Muzzle Up

There may be times that the shooter may want to carry the shotgun in a muzzle up fashion. For muzzle up, the gun is carried in a way that looks much like the "port arms" military carry.

Once more, the dominant hand is controlling the gun by holding the grip area. The support hand is on the forend/slide portion.

The receiver of the shotgun is again rotated just as with the muzzle down. Ejection port out for right handers, ejection port in for left handers.

To address a target from the muzzle up carry, the first action will be to drive the muzzle toward the target while simultaneously disengaging the manual safety. Think of it as if you have a bayonet on your gun and you are trying to point that bayonet at the center of the enemy's chest.

The aforementioned action will put the butt of the stock in a position that is in line with the shoulder pocket but a few inches forward. The moment the shotgun is pointed out and level with the shoulder pocket, we pull it back into the proper mount position and fire if needed.

There is a valid reason for thrusting the gun out and pulling it back in as opposed to trying to sweep the butt stock up from the waist to your shoulder. If you are wearing a jacket, vest, load bearing gear, or even just a long sleeve shirt with pockets, there is a good chance that the stock will catch or snag on the way to the mount position. An additional important reason to "thrust and pull" is that this motion will put the buttstock right into the place it is supposed to be in the shoulder pocket. This action is repeatable and creates a consistent mount. Consistency in the mount is one of the keys to success with a shotgun.

Whether muzzle up or muzzle down, the point of the exercise is to be constantly conscious of where your muzzle is pointed. You must develop a natural muzzle awareness where all are always pointing the gun where it needs to be. This might be the ground, the sky or a deadly threat. And, yes, both muzzle up and muzzle down can be correct for the situation.

**Muzzle Up Carry**

### *Sling Carry*

During GWOT, when shotguns were being employed in combat like no time before in recent history, sling and accessory makers came up with many new and wild ways to affix slings to long guns. The single-point sling came into vogue for the M4 and its many variants. Some companies came up with single-point sling attachments for shotguns, particularly for the Benelli M4 used by the Marine Corps.

The two-point sling is hundreds of years old, going back to flintlock muskets. One end of the sling is affixed forward, near the muzzle, and the second part is attached to the buttstock. This is simple and easy to use and has stood the test of time.

The primary purpose of the sling, whether single or double point, is to act as a kind of holster for a long gun. The sling allows the user to employ both hands without the need to set the gun down somewhere. From a tactical standpoint, this is naturally a valid concern. Setting your primary weapon down and walking away to perform a task is not a good idea in a tactical or combat environment.

Minus a sling, when a single hand is required for a task, the support hand controls the gun and the shooter uses their dominant hand. In a tactical environment, If two hands are required, the weapon should be staged so that the user can retrieve it by taking no more than one big step.

When I was a police officer I never once encountered a cruiser shotgun that had a sling attached to it. The thought process was that the gun would only be grabbed when a fight was at hand and also that a sling would get caught on the inside of the police car. When I carried a shotgun aboard a naval vessel for shipboard security, these guns were also void of slings. Getting caught up in a close quarters environment of a ship was one reason and readiness was another. Our Marine officers wanted us to patrol with both hands controlling the shotgun so it was ready to deploy at a moment's notice.

If you are going to be using a shotgun as your primary weapon outdoors and engaging in foot patrols, guard duty or some similar task, a two-point sling is a valid and valuable option. Let's consider the primary ways we will carry a fighting shotgun with a sling.

### African Carry

When I was in the Marine Corps, one First Sergeant, a Vietnam combat veteran, taught us what he called the "South African Carry" for the shotgun. The shorter, popular term is simply *African Carry.*

For the African Carry method, the shotgun is carried on the support side shoulder with the support hand controlling the forend/slide portion of the gun and the muzzle pointed down. When the gun is needed, the support hand pulls the gun up, rotating the shotgun to direct the butt to the shoulder pocket. As the support hand is rotating the shotgun, the dominant hand comes up and grabs the grip portion. The stock is driven into the mount position as the safety is disengaged by the dominant hand.

With practice, the shotgun can go from this administrative, muzzle down position, up to a firing position very quickly; think one to two seconds from slung to mounted. Naturally, the African Carry works with rifles as well.

**African sling carry**

### American Carry or Parade Sling

The next sling carry method has been referred to both as the American Carry or the Parade Sling method. We have all seen pictures or videos of soldiers marching with rifles slung over their dominant side shoulder with the muzzle pointing up. I suppose we could also call this the hunter carry method as well. In the American or Parade carry position, the dominant hand controls the shotgun by holding onto the sling itself about midway up and down.

To go from Parade Sling carry to mount on target, the shooter will reach up under the dominant side arm and grab a hold of the forend with their support hand. The dominant hand releases the sling as the support hand pulls the gun around the dominant arm. The now freed dominant hand grabs the grip. To mount the gun we will execute the thrust/pull method of driving the muzzle forward and then the butt back into the shoulder pocket. During this process the dominant hand has disengaged the manual safety and the gun is ready to fire on target.

As you can imagine, of all the ways to get on target for a shot, the American or Parade Sling carry method is the most time consuming. How much time is consumed? Perhaps two or three seconds. The more often the shooter trains, the smoother and more efficient the movement will become. Does two or three seconds make a difference? I suppose that depends on whether or not someone has decided to start shooting at you.

**American/Parade sling carry**

## Training for the Real World

All of the above; muzzle up or down, sling or no sling, must be trained and practiced on the range if we have any hope of being able to do the right thing under the stress of real world deadly encounters.

During the aftermath of natural or manmade disasters, dudes will grab their shotguns from their closets and decide they are going to "pull security" for their community or neighborhood. That is admirable. The unfortunate and very real situation is that most of these well-intentioned folks have little or no training. There is a huge difference between using a shotgun on the trap range or shooting doves and moving around other people with a loaded weapon in your hands.

During a crisis you have enough to worry about without having to worry that your kindly neighbor, Jim, is going to negligently shoot someone because they have never actually carried a loaded gun off of the skeet range.

The idea that people will "rise to the occasion" or will simply just do what is right because there is a disaster or a crisis is naive and dangerous. During a crisis you will behave and perform however you have been trained and you will only rise to the level of training that you have mastered. This is the reason why we must master on the training range all of the potential ways and situations in which we might be expected to perform.

Going back to our previous discussion of folks who never chamber a round until they "think they might need it". If you have a person who has never carried or trained with a chamber loaded shotgun, but during a crisis they think that they should load the chamber, that person is a dangerous hazard. Having never practiced disengaging the manual safety, during the adrenaline dump of a deadly force encounter, they will forget to take the safety off or they will be afraid that they might forget and they will walk around with the gun loaded, safety off, "just in case" they need to use it quickly.

# Chapter 6 Specialty Items

I am hesitant to even begin this chapter as the wild variety of special items and loads for the 12 gauge shotgun has contributed to the confusion and mythology surrounding the tool. However, as this is a book and books are supposed to be about education and information, I will venture forth with caution.

**Less-than-Lethal?**

One of the biggest myths or misunderstandings surrounds the modern shotgun is the use of supposed "less-than-lethal" specialty shells. This type of ammunition was originally designed with law enforcement and corrections officers in mind to deal with civil disturbances and prison riots. However, various less-than-lethals have made their way into the citizen marketplace.

The first thing that you need to understand is that, from a legal standpoint, a shotgun is a firearm. Loading rubber buckshot or "bean bag" shells into a 12G shotgun does not magically make it not a firearm. Pointing a firearm at a human, threatening to use a firearm, or discharging a firearm, all fall under the legal definition of "deadly force". The legal or justifiable use of deadly force must meet certain criteria. If all of those criteria are not met and you point a shotgun at a human being or threaten them with a shotgun, you are now committing a felony.

If you cannot demonstrate that deadly force was justified, it makes no difference whatsoever what kind of shell was loaded in your shotgun. As I mentioned, a shotgun is always a *firearm* by legal definition and you cannot just arbitrarily point a shotgun at someone because they annoyed you or made you mad.

If the deadly force criteria are not present, threatening someone with a shotgun makes you the criminal. On the other hand, if you are indeed being threatened with deadly force, why in the name of all that is Holy would you want to use rubber pellets or bean bags? Also, depending on the distance, both rubber pellets and bean bag rounds can be lethal or deadly. Remember; "Deadly force is that force which causes or is likely to cause death or serious bodily injury".

I am personally aware of an instance in a prison where a guard was surprised by an inmate who attacked him at close range. The guard fired his special, bean-bag loaded shotgun from a distance of less than a yard. The "less-than-lethal" bean bag entered the inmate's right cheek, smashed about half of his teeth and exited out the left side of his face. The corrections officer who related the story to me referred to the results as "gruesome".

My primary point regarding supposed "less-than-lethal" shotgun shells is that you are either deliberately putting yourself at a tactical disadvantage or you are putting yourself in position to be charged by a hostile prosecutor with "Assault with a Deadly Weapon", "Aggravated Menacing", "Aggravated Assault" etc. Unless you are a police officer or work in corrections, there are far better less-than-lethal options.

Also, this is not 1885 where you can get away with shooting watermelon thieves with rock salt. If you fire a shotgun, even loaded with rock salt, at a person and the deadly force criteria are not present, it is you who will be going to prison.

## Kitchen Sink Loads

By this I mean, "everything but the kitchen sink" going back to "I threw everything at him but the kitchen sink." If you have never heard that, go ask your dad or grandfather. There are numerous loads, most of them being crazy expensive compared to standard ammunition, that contain all manner of objects: flechettes (tiny steel darts), "dumbbell" double ended slugs, BB's mixed with buckshot, buckshot mixed with slugs, steel balls attached to one another with a piece of cable, there is even a load this filled with steel metal shavings (we can only guess they swept them up from around a CNC machine).

As far as I can tell, the entire purpose of all of these "kitchen sink loads" is to convince you to pay from $4-6 PER SHOT depending on which ones you choose. The mythology is that your shotgun is somehow now more lethal than it would be with the boring old 1 ¼ ounce Foster slugs or nine 00 buckshot pellets.

Here is the reality, either buckshot or slug ammunition from reputable manufacturers with long standing track records for quality control are far better choices than exotic or specialty rounds that are produced in hundreds or merely dozens.

As we discussed in an earlier section, part of the preparation phase for employing a fighting shotgun is to practice and train with the ammunition you will be loading for the potential fight. For buckshot, we need to pattern it to understand exactly how it will perform from our specific gun. With slugs you need to know where they are going to be striking and make adjustments if necessary. What kind of QA and consistency go into the 3 packs of exotic ammunition? When it comes to betting your life on the performance of a gun and ammunition, I would advise sticking with companies that have centuries of experience producing their wares.

**Valuable Specialty Loads**

Federal Cartridge produces a line of "reduced recoil" shotgun ammunition in buckshot with what they call a "flight controlling" wad. This ammunition, despite being "reduced recoil" still chronographs at 1250 feet per second. The flight control wads produce tremendously consistent, tight, and reliable patterns. I have used it for some time and can vouch for the quality. This falls in their "Premium Personal Defense" line of shotgun ammo.

As this book goes to print, Federal has another new load, the "Force X2". This 12 gauge ammunition uses specially designed 00 copper-plated buckshot. The Force X2 00 buck is pre-split in the factory. Each piece of 00 buck flies as one piece but breaks into two equal pieces on impact.

**Federal 00 Buck and Winchester Slugs**

Winchester Ammunition introduced a product several years ago called the "Segmented Rifled Slug". The engineering genius in this design is that they took a tried and true lead Foster-type slug and pre-segmented it. The slug flies straight to the target as a single projectile, however, when it meets resistance *(strikes flesh)* it comes apart in three equal segments.

The year this load was introduced, I took a Remington 870 and the Winchester segmented slugs to Texas and dropped a 175 pound feral hog at 75 yards with it. The hog did not take more than one step after impact and all three pieces stayed inside of its body. I cannot recommend this ingenious product highly enough. PS: This slug flies at 1600 feet per second out of the muzzle.

One of the many types of training I underwent as a police officer was dynamic breaching. During the training program, among other things, we used a 12 gauge shotgun as an entry tool to breach barricades, etc. The ammunition we used were specially designed frangible slugs. The projectiles for such ammunition are made by using compressed zinc or copper powder with a binding agent to hold it together.

A frangible shotgun slug flies as a single projectile, but when it meets resistance, it comes apart and disintegrates on impact. This type of ammunition is also used for training against steel targets as there is little to no danger of large lead fragments injuring the shooter or other good guys. Frangible shotgun shells are indeed a specialty product, but they fall into the extremely valuable and useful category for their specific mission.

Author's Note: Shotgun breaching is a unique or special skill and requires more training than a typical fighting shotgun. However, this is one case where the versatility of a 12 gauge shotgun shines.

**Stand Off muzzle device for breaching, affixed to the Mossberg 930 Tactical shotgun.**

## Short Shells / Mini-Shells

Aguila Ammunition of Mexico was the first company to introduce a 1 and ¾ inch 12 gauge shotshell. These come in birdshot, buckshot, and 5/8 ounce slug configuration. Challenger ammunition came up with their own version of the "shorty" as did Federal Ammunition recently. These short shells have been known colloquially as "hater tots".

I have been using the "shorty" shells for several years with great success on the range and in the field. The birdshot shells are great for varmints and pest animals. The only downside is that the short shells will not cycle in all 12 gauge guns, particularly semi-autos. The buckshot and slug shells might not seem as *powerful* as a standard shell, but I'm guessing 5/8 ounces (273 grains) of lead at 1300 feet per second will get a felon's attention. Federal makes the Force X2 in a mini-shell with 6 specially designed 00 buckshot pellets.

**Federal Premium Shorties or "Hater-tots"**

## Add-on Accessories

*White Light*

Most fighting shotguns are ready to go with no additions from the factory. There are dozens if not hundreds of ridiculous and pointless products you can strap onto a shotgun, however, one that is useful and makes sense is a specially designed forend that incorporates a built-in white light.

Despite what the Meat Puppet named Joe once said on national TV, we cannot legally or morally fire a shotgun at scary sounds or shadows. Before you press the trigger on your shotgun, you must be absolutely certain of your target. How do we do that in the dark? We shine a bright white light on the subject. Surefire and Streamlight are the top producers of shotgun forends that have bright white LED flashlights built into them.

There are other ways to affix a light to a shotgun, but most require you to take your support hand off of the forend to use them. There are also techniques to hold a handheld light with firing your shotgun, but again, function of the gun is hampered.

*Shotgun Sights*

The industry standard for fighting shotguns is to install a brass bead front sight just above the muzzle. This sight design is easily a century or more old and it has worked for as long. From an industry standpoint the difference between a "field barrel" and a "slug barrel" is not only the length, but the sights. Slug barrels come with "rifle sights", that is, an adjustable rear sight and a corresponding front sight blade of some sort.

Do you need a front and rear sight on your fighting shotgun? I suppose it depends on your definition of *need.* I have found that Foster slugs *(remember, they are rifled)* will strike the center chest of a humanoid target at standard fighting distances out to 25 yards using just a bead sight and a smooth, 18 inch barrel. There is certainly nothing wrong with having sights on your combat shotgun. However, you should not feel like you are handicapped without them.

There are numerous types and styles of front sights that you can install on your shotgun, from large brass beads, to white marbles, to colored fiber optics, even Tritium. Depending on which you might choose, you may or may not need a gunsmith to install them. A word of caution regarding fiber optic sights. The fiber optic material is super bright in the sunlight when it is new. However, the recoil from every shot will put tiny, microscopic cracks in the fiber optic material and over time it will lose much or most of its light gathering capability. Fiber optics sights are meant to be changed out after so much use. If you never plan to change your fiber optic sight, you might pick another option.

**Standard brass bead sight**

**Front rifle sight on Rem 870**

**Rear rifle sight on Rem 870**

*Red Dot Sights*

Most modern shotguns have receivers that are pre-tapped from the factory to accept some type of optic rail. Installing a Picatinny style rail on a Mossberg or Remington shotgun can be done easily on your workbench. Perhaps your gun came with a rail already mounted from the factory. Great, you are ahead of the game.

While some traditionalists view the addition of an optics sight to a shotgun as wasteful overkill or unnecessary, the idea has serious merit. First, we must remember that the addition of any sight, optic, or scope to a firearm does absolutely nothing to alter the mechanical accuracy that was built into the gun. The sight is not for the gun, the sight is for the shooter. More specifically, the sight is there to aid the shooter's eyes, their vision. When I was a young Marine Recruit on the Parris Island Rifle Range, I could see the black front sight of my M16A2 rifle with crystal clarity in normal light. I could even make out the ever so slight machine marks on the thin black post. Today, that is no longer the case.

The benefits of a 1:1 optical sight on a shotgun, be it red or one of the newer bright green reticles, is that it allows the shooter to not only find the aiming device in all light conditions, it is also adjustable from low to high to compensate for the shooter's vision.

Additionally, when shooting single projectiles *(slugs)* the optic can be easily zeroed to practical ranges such as 25 or 50 yards. If your desire is to take long shots, beyond 100 yards, you should just use a rifle instead.

As with our discussion of rifle style sights on a shotgun, your definition of *need* will vary. I know men who used to think that an optic on a shotgun was overkill and then after trying out a gun with a 1:1 red dot swore that they would never go back.

One of the biggest benefits to adding a red or green 1:1 optic to a shotgun is shooter confidence. Shooters who have a zeroed optic, even if they are using buckshot, have reported that when they placed the dot on the target they "knew" that it would be a good shot the moment the trigger broke. From a trainer's perspective, I have witnessed new shooters move faster through the learning curve when using electronic dot sights.

For those who might say, "Well, what if the battery dies or the sight stops working?" If that is the case, you are right back where you started and you are no more handicapped than if you were using a brass bead.

*Pistol Grips and AR Stocks*

One of the modern options that has become vogue or cool over the last twenty years or so is to add a pistol grip and some type of AR or M4 style stock to traditional combat shotguns. A vertical pistol grip on any long gun offers the advantage of greater control of the gun, particularly when controlling it with the dominant hand.

The detriment that I noticed from the very beginning with the straight, retractable M4 style stocks is that the shooter's face/cheek winds up lower than with a traditional fixed shotgun stock. What happens invariably is that a lower stockweld causes the shooter to unconsciously elevate the muzzle of the gun. The result is a shot pattern that strikes high. How high and at what distance? From distances as close as ten yards I have noticed shot patterns flying right over a prairie dog or ground squirrel. Remember, the closer you are to the target, the tighter the pattern and the more important a good aim/stockweld becomes.

The solution that most people will apply when they realize their shot patterns are high with one of these pistol grip stock shotguns is to hold low or put the bead at the base of the target. That is one way to go about it. The other way is to install a 1:1 dot optic and simply tune the dot so that the patterns or slugs are striking point of aim/point of impact.

# Chapter 7 Sporting Guns and the Shockwave

## Sporting Guns

Of the tens of millions of shotguns sold by Mossberg and Remington, many of these were produced as sporting guns. By sporting guns, we are primarily talking about the guns with long or extra long barrels. While a 22, 24, or even 28 inch barrel might offer an advantage when shooting birds or clay targets, extra long barrels add weight and bulk to the gun. In the field, that doesn't matter much, in a fighting situation it does.

The good news is that both the Mossberg 500 series and the Remington 870 series allow for easy, workbench swapping of barrels without the need for special tools. Both Mossberg and Remington offer 18 inch barrels for sale as options. If you have a field gun and want to use it as a fighting tool, rather than purchase another gun, you can buy an additional barrel for about half of what it would cost for a new gun.

Another consideration with sporting guns is that many of them have historically been shipped from the factory with "plugs" in the magazine tubes to limit the number of shells in order to meet various hunting regulations. The good news here is that these plugs can be easily removed by disassembling the gun. I have personally removed these limiters on several occasions.

Most fighting shotguns are essentially modified versions of sporting shotguns anyway. One of the big benefits of using a combat shotgun from Remington or Mossberg is the plethora of spare parts, stocks and furniture that are available.

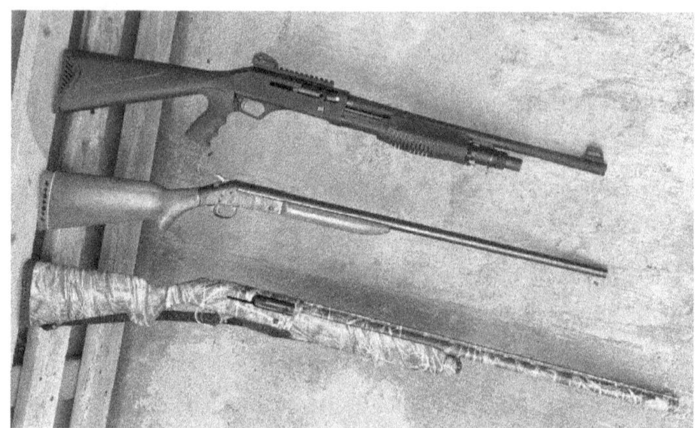

**Various shotguns: fighting and sport**

## The Shockwave

Remington was first on the market with a 14 inch barreled "firearm" with a "birdshead" grip. This model is called the TAC-14. It is NOT an NFA item and can be purchased like any normal firearm. The Remington model has a steel receiver and holds 4+1 standard 2 and ¾ inch shells. The overall length is 26.5 inches and it weighs 6.2 pounds empty.

Fast on the heels of Remington, Mossberg introduced The Shockwave. The Shockwave has a birdshead grip and an aluminum receiver. Since its introduction, Mossberg has added numerous models to their Shockwave line. The basic model has a 14 inch barrel, an overall length of 26.37 inches and weighs 5.25 pounds empty.

Because of the popularity of the Mossberg Shockwave, all of the birdshead guns have become known as "Shockwaves", much like all brands of tissue are referred to as Kleenex.

As far as the AFT is concerned, these guns are not shotguns but "firearms". You can call them Rumpelstiltskin if you like, what they are are super handy, tremendously useful guns that chamber 12 gauge ammunition.

In their stock configuration, the birdshead guns are useful and practical, however, with the addition of a stabilizing brace from SB Tactical, they become extremely practical fighting tools. While some purists have poo-pooed the Shockwave, I can tell you that the handling characteristics of a 14 inch gun are superb. This is one of those things that you really need to try or experience to understand.

When it comes to the martial application of a shotgun, a short gun such as the Shockwave loses none of the punch or effectiveness. Due to the popularity of the mini-shells, Mossberg recently introduced a new version called the 590S. The 590S has a modified shell elevator allowing it to feed and cycle shells in the 1 ¾, 2 ¾, and 3 inch varieties.

The 590S Shockwave gun will hold 8+1 rounds of the mini-shells. That is a lot of ammo in a compact package. If you have an older model Shockwave and wish to run the mini-shells in it, you will need to add an adapter from a Texas company called OpSol. I have been using an

OpSol Mini-Clip in my original Shockwave for years and the little shells cycle flawlessly.

The Shockwave guns from Mossberg also have a nylon strap on the forend to keep the shooter's hand in place. This is a good feature and there is not any detriment to it.

I have limited experience with the Remington TAC-14 having only shot it a few times. I can tell you that it will not cycle the mini-shells. The TAC-14 is based upon the 870 action so it is tried and true. If you must have a steel receiver gun, choose the Remington. If you want less weight, choose the Mossberg.

**Shockwave with SB Tactical Brace**

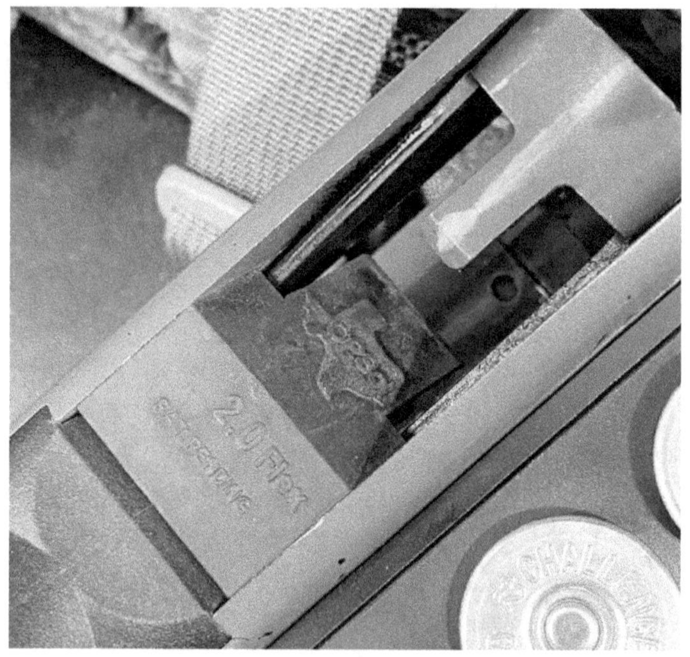

**The Op Sol adapter in the Shockwave
allows the mini-shells to cycle flawlessly.**

**Mossberg 590S is designed to feed shells from 1 ¾" to 3" with no additional modifications required.**

**New shell elevator on the 590S**

# Parting Shots

As you can tell or should have realized by the time that you got to this part, a fighting shotgun is not as simple of a tool as one might have been led to believe. Yes, there are thousands upon thousands of people who will buy a shotgun "just in case", stick it in the closet with the idea that they will use it as you would a fire extinguisher in an emergency.

During a conversation with one acquaintance, he related to me that during the recent spate of riots he had gone out and bought a shotgun for "home defense". When I asked him what he thought about the gun, the man stated matter-of-factly that he had never shot it. He related that he loaded rounds into the magazine tube and staged it in his bedroom closet. "You can't miss with a shotgun." he said to me as if explaining it to a five year old.

Such people, if ever faced with a life and death attack might get lucky. Then again, they might not. When it comes to what my friend Massad Ayoob calls "The Gravest Extreme", betting your life on *probably* or hoping that you will be *lucky* is both naive and reckless. When it comes to the subject of a home defense gun, you are not just defending your life, you are defending the lives of your spouse and your children. What if you are not lucky and in a panicked state you cannot make the gun work? Who defends your family while you lie bleeding in the hallway because you never practiced pumping the action or taking off the safety lever?

Going back to the beginning, a fighting shotgun is a ferocious and powerful fight-stopping tool when used at the close ranges of personal combat. The martial application of the shotgun is meant to be the sledgehammer that destroys whatever is threatening you and your loved ones.

Yes, a 12 gauge combat shotgun is a ferocious guard dog, but there is no magic to it. If you hope to use that tool swiftly and effectively when your life is threatened, you must put in the time. The good news is that if you do decide to put in the time and train with the shotgun, you can become good with it and then someday, with enough effort, master the tool. My hope for you is that this book has inspired you to do just that.

For more information regarding training: Please go to www.SOTGU.com

**Additional Books from the Author**

- Student of the Gun Instructor Development Manual

- Precision Rifle Range Book

- Martial Application of the Pistol

- Patriot Fire Team Manual

- Patriot Fire Team Equipment Guide

- Patriot Fire Team Mission Planner

**Mr. Markel's professional education includes:**

- Executive Security International
  - Executive Protection and Bodyguard studies
  - Intelligence Gathering and Investigation
  - Advanced Firearms training under John S. Farnam

- **United States Marine Corps** service training  *Combat Decorated Veteran*
  - Basic Training: Physical Fitness, Rifle Marksmanship, Swim Qualification, First Aid, Marine Corps History and Traditions
  - School of the Infantry: Anti-Tank Assault, Patrolling, Ambush Techniques, Nighttime and Low Light Operations
  - Sea Service Indoctrination School: Shipboard Firefighting and Damage Control, Naval Service traditions, Advanced Physical Training, Advanced Marksmanship Training, Customs and Courtesies
  - Shipboard Security Engagement Training (SSET) and Nuclear Weapons Storage and Security School, Fast Reaction Team training

- o Demolitions, Mines and Explosive Ordnance School
  - o USMC Marksmanship Coaches School
  - o Desert Survival Training
  - o Jungle Warfare Indoctrination and Patrolling
  - o USMC Leadership Training / NCO Course

- Ohio State Peace Officers Academy (State Police Academy)

- Special Weapons and Tactics Manual Structure Breaching School

- Advanced Firearms Training Courses
  - o Gunsite Academy: Rifle, Pistol, Shotgun courses
  - o Tactical Defense Institute: Close Quarters Fighting, Pistol, and Rifle courses
  - o SIG Academy: Pistol, Carbine, Shotgun, Long Range Rifle courses
  - o Tactical Response: Fighting Pistol and Fighting Rifle, Close Quarters Fighting courses, Fight Strong Strength Training

- o Ken Hackathorn: Advanced Handgun and Carbine Course
  - o International Tactical Training Systems: Urban Sniper School
  - o Blackwater Academy: Advanced Shotgun course
  - o Expeditionary Combat Skills: Advanced Rifle and Pistol, Tactical Combat Casualty Care, Judgment-based Engagement Training

- Instructor Courses
  - o SureFire Academy: Low Light Tactics Instructor School
  - o U.S.M.C. Marksmanship Coaches School
  - o U.S. Navy Marksmanship Coaches School
  - o Tidewater Community College Instructor Training Course
  - o Oleoresin Capsicum Aerosol Training Instructor Trainer School
  - o Red Cross CPR and Family First Aid Instructor course
  - o National Rifle Association: Handgun, Rifle, and Shotgun Instructor School, Range Safety Officers School,

- NRA Law Enforcement Handgun and Shotgun Instructor school
- National 4H Youth Firearms Instructors School

Mr. Markel has been teaching safe and effective firearms handling to students young and old for decades and has worked actively with the 4-H Shooting Sports program. Paul holds numerous instructor certifications in multiple disciplines; nonetheless, he is and will remain a dedicated Student of the Gun.